CONNECTS

VOSHAWN T. WHITE

TABLE OF CONTENTS

LETTER FROM THE AUTHOR

Dear Reader,

We've finally reached the end of this poetry trilogy.

I had no intension of publishing another book so soon, making two in one year. But when the creative urge took over, I just had to get everything together for this concept of poems, while I had them in my head.

Just a quick recap, my poetry journey began a few years back, when I needed to express a lot of feelings during a period where I tried numerous ways to express myself from feeling numb. Writing poetry seemed to be the number one thing that stuck.

Fast forward a few years later, these past few months of my creative process I've learned a lot about myself and my creative writing process. Like I enjoy writing on Sundays and Wednesdays. I normally enjoy the presence of a carnelian stone in my writing space. To help boost self-esteem and passion for what I'm writing. And most recently I've enjoyed traveling to newer places to help develop newer ideas for inspiration. I took a few days to go off on a writing retreat to Massachusetts (Boston and Salem). To help 'connect' more with myself, my creative powers and higher creativity Gods. While on this unplugged adventure I felt so inspired. And it was there that I realized, during many hours of alone time and writing, the true nature of my creative process that has reflected in my previous books. I developed a diagram (see next page) that reflects how I feel the general creative process goes, which reflected on my books.

"Moments" the first stage, which is the starting point. This base is what happens when you literally experience a thought or event that happens in that particular....moment.

"Sideshows" the second stage, which represents the scary journeys you must take to get to the final outcome.

"Connects" the third and final stage. Which is arriving, things coming full-circle and finally 'connecting' to the idea. To share and shine it into fruition.

Last thing I'd like to say is, everything is 'connected'. And when you read these poems and mentally go to this final place I've set up, full of final ideas I've created, I hope you all experience some type of connection with me, the world and other people.

I hope you've enjoyed this ride we've been on together.

V.T.W.

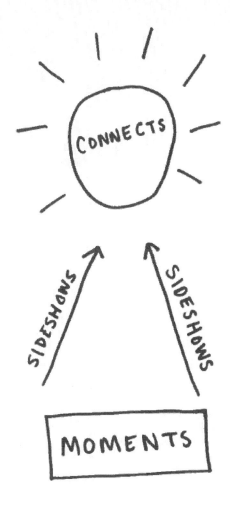

Clockwise

Time is ticking

And it starts when we're infants

We rotate through seasons,

Through light and darkness

Through joy and sorrow

Through growth and decay

Moments layered upon moments

Passing by the sideshows

on our journey to the destination,

the center.

A tiny, pulsing core moving clockwise

Forcing all destined outcomes.

Everything that's meant to happen

Will happen no matter what

Yet even as we reach

The outermost rim

We remained connected

To the center, to the source

Saudade

I ran away from you to the 80's

And I ran, I ran so far away

I missed life as a teenager

Watching MTV on the loose

But I felt everyone's eyes on me

like I didn't belong

You see I'm a 90's kid, so

I was in over my head

Our love had been a battlefield for a while

No weapons, just tears

The same tears doves cried

When I made peace

And decided to come back

Even hiding in the past

Didn't give me enough camouflage

To face the problems we share today

I'd like to go back someday

Maybe for an extended Roman Holiday

I've found this Portuguese word to help

Understanding my heart's weary pain

Lucky Charm

I can't let you go

I'll follow you near

My gentle little guide

That banishes fear

A magnificent inspiration

A psychedelic sensation

The four leaf clover

I always pray over

Every step,

You pave the way

To help bring light

On the shadowy days

Goodluck's blessing

That's mine to keep

A permanent smile

I'll wear in my sleep.

Things to Fix

A crooked smile

That hints at pain

Eyes are drooping

With exhaustion's stain

Skin that's marred,

By life's rough hand

Hair that's tangled

In an unruly stand

A mind that wonders

With no creative spark

Like all hopes and dreams

Fading into the dark

All the things I'd fix

Don't really matter

Since all minds

Love to play tricks

Coffee Buddies

Call me crazy

For talking to plants

Normal people walk by them

Without even giving a glance

They whisper neighbor's secrets,

Out on my patio

The latest drama from the couple

next door

Is their favorite running

reality television show.

Early Sunday Mornings

I'm a therapist without warning

"This spot is too hot"

"Please refill my pot"

"Do we get water today or not?"

These friends of mine,

they always make me smile

Even if sanity

Keeps me in denial

Sleeper, Stay Asleep

Every night

I'm channeling you

Calling out to the past

To make sure you're ok

You haven't met me yet

And that's ok

Look down at your left arm

We share the same birthmark

So you can trust me

You've always been sneaky

Thinking you're one step ahead

And it's ok to:

Thank your mother

The Queen of a bright smile

For handing you down glamour

For handing you down craftsmanship

She encourages your individuality

Thank your father

The King of self-sacrifice

For passing you down resilience

For passing you down humor

He encourages your hard work

Thank yourself

For letting your creativity grow

With over 100 copies

Of Sideshows sold.

On your journey

You'll lose your hair

You'll lose your ego

You'll lose your patience

You'll gain more wisdom

You'll gain more security

You'll gain more love

Follow that light in the night

That moves through the trees

To wherever

Your creativity guides you next

Sweet dreams, VoShawn

And stay asleep

Let your imagination wonder

As you see,

You can be anything

You choose to be

Halo of Salt

My seven letter name

Is my protection

My Haint Blue ceilings

Paint the air, I breathe

All the souls of yesterday

On stand by

I count myself lucky

in many ways

I count myself thankful

in more ways

The roots from the past

Stretch up my spine

And hover over my head

Chrysalis

Our minds are a private place

Our minds are always changing

The thought process is slow

Stagnant

No passionate next move

The thought process is painful

Bruised

Chaotic trying to calm down

The thought process is beautiful

Delightful

Knowing you're good enough

Silent Fishing

A peaceful hush

Softly wraps the world's busy rush

As dawn approaches,

I cast my line

Not to fish, but for my inner peace

My thoughts clear away;

a new day to embrace

The warm colors in my mind

Help calm my internal space

Obstacles are tugging and jerking

But I keep a tough skin.

Cause I catch them and simply

Toss them back in

The frantic world slows down

From it's pace

As dusk approaches,

Serenity takes place

Quicksand

Mother nature's embrace

Has always been a fragile hold

A human's grasp

For centuries has been too bold

Resources dwindle down

Like shifting sand

A delicate balance,

Lost to our demands.

Sand tickles our feet

Slowly pulling us deep

As our forest vanishes

and oceans start to creep.

Our peace has been stolen

And left out to dry

Like a cracked riverbend

No water to supply

Yet we still take

With a blinded eye

Ignoring the songs

As earth says goodbye.

The hourglass is almost out

Bringing on more doubt.

Will we be saved

From Nature's harsh voice?

Or sink forever

In our selfish choice?

Feeding the Fire

I am the warrior

Battling and defending all my emotions

On top of Mount Olympus

Causing wreckage and commotion

A flame that grows

From a hungry stomach

Causing my roar

Vibrating off cave walls

Shaking my heart to its core

My enemy's cry

From my triumph win

Sends chills and goosebumps

Across my ashy skin

My heart makes a beat

And the flame reignites

Resetting my brain

Causing another primal fight

Falling on my back

I call out to Mars

But all I hear are echoes,

Bouncing back from the stars

I must keep fighting

For the hungry flame

I must keep fighting

For my family's name

Washing the Water

I am the healer

Pushing and pulling ripples all anew

In the Tropic of Cancer

Like a hurricane has grew

I stand at the edge

With my hands immersed

Washing the water

As tears dispersed

I rinse the residue of the past

And let all those worries

Just sail away

In this liquid lap

I cleanse our souls

A baptism of peace

That makes us all whole

The water's song

A gentle hush

Vibrates my own spirit

In it's soothing rush

Light like my heart

it slips through my fingers

Light like my heart

the memories do not linger

Counterclockwise

Time is ticking

And since it's man made

We're able to pull the hands back

In a reversible speed

To retrace our steps

That lets us cheat death

The art of starting over

Begging for second chances

In a cycle of redemptions

In picking up lost pieces

Using the knowledge we know

To make our future brighter

If time travel was real

And the ability to redo

Would we ever learn our lesson

Would we ever take blame

Sun In Our Eyes

On a distant world

I see your face from miles away

The sun rays shine down on our faces

Where love is born

In each other's eyes

Our hearts reside,

We stroll through the valleys

Carved by ancient rivers

Climb the mountains

That make ancient secrets quiver

Helping our love grow strong

Wishing were in each other's arms

A place that feels like home

To help transcend this planet's unknown

Everything around us shines bright and true

A beacon in the darkness

Guiding me and you.

Now the sun begins to set

And our love still paints the skies

Belladonna Supernova

Oh dear, stop your crying

Can't you see the world around you

Is dying

The galaxy is your playground

And you skip around like a comet.

A white rose in the snow, still grows

Except you're like Christmas

With no gifts

Oh dear, stop your crying

Words that slip from your lips

Are gaslighting

Purple hydrangeas in your hair

Similar to Medusa's snakes

Evil to the stare

Did you look in the mirror

To turn your heart to stone

Or are you just comfortable

Being left alone

Oh dear, stop your crying

Cause when you burst it'll

Be electrifying

With those red poppy eyes

Dropping tears down

And causing craters all over

You think you have a soul

But it's just a black hole

99 Quartz

I've spent ninety-nine days

Holding a glass jar

With an open lid

Up to the sun

Trying to catch the light

Eating the Earth

I am the consumer

Ready to digest the dark richness

Setting the table at Stonehenge

Tree roots matching my veins

Forks and knives in my hands

Dirt between my teeth

Nourishing my appetite

I devour the land

Not for greed or might

But for resurgence

On every bite

This has become a sacred union

For Mother Nature and me

The rocks our witnesses

The bugs our guest

All life forms of family trees

That make up the past's history

Thankful for the nutrients

She always provides

This binding contract

Gives me no choice

By eating the earth

I become its voice

Weaving the Wind

I am the designer

Attempting to express myself

In the palace of Versailles

Trying to show my vision

Waving my hands in the air

Sculpting together patterns

Finding it hard for others

To see my masterpieces

For they're all blind

To the naked eye

Each strand of imagination

Intertwined with precise care

Colorless textures sewing anew

The big empty space

So much potential to create.

I can hear them applauding

The beauty, the passion

From the work

Of my delicate hands

Constructing breezes

That come in down below

With creativity in the wind

Beginning to blow

Trinket

Syad tsekrad eht no senihs taht

Tekcop ruoy ni

Esolc dloh nac uoy that gnihtemos

Rehto on ekil evila leef ouy sekam

Taht gnihtemos gnivah si

Devil efil lluf

A

my dreams of stepping barefoot on broken sounds

Listen,

I was born sensitive

Can't you hear it

From head to toes

My front lobe glows

Eyes closed tight

Mind wide open

Static tv on demand

Open palm and hands

I've been here before

Both cracking and shatter

Vile yellow and purple

Back to where

All things are uneven

Broken and unbothered

Freckles all smooth together

Arm hair salutes sides

Left foot down

Right foot down

Eyes still closed

Bleeding ears exposed

I feel it shatter

Between my toes

Unspoken euphoria

Pluto's Return

An unknown due date

Protecting her nest

A waiting room

In limbo

Unconditional

Love to come

Guardian

Of new life

An unknown due date

He sleeps.

Brothers and sisters

Together

Cradled and bundled

Into a soft,

Humid lullaby

He's done this

All before

Holographic and Unseen

We're phantom twins

Finally set free

Seeds of childhood uprooted

Technicolor smiles

Strings that are cut

Spring has finally sprung

My long feet have blisters

While I dance with the world

After the Storm

Wild winds may return

Over again to do damage

I'll face them unbroken

Calm and collected

My voice clear

My heart steadfast

Striking conversations

Like a lightning bolt

Cause after the storm

Find me under the rainbow

Never under the weather

Writing away

Never looking back

Always going clockwise

Just like Maya Angelou

Still I'll rise

Nomad

In the silence I hear my soul

A whispered truth

A wondering goal

Heart beating fast in my chest

Compulsive to find the next place to rest

On the dusty ground

I roam without a sound

No fixed abode

No settled nest

My home is wherever

My feet find rest

Far away, I hear them say

Stars above a twinkling sea

Trying to find my real destiny

A hunger for the unknown

Never staying long

Never quite a part

I'll follow the wind

Where it whispers my name

I'll never feel the same

Happily Ever After

Since my birth

Society chose me to fail

For my skin tone, my income

And being attracted to another male

Whispers from distances

Feeding my head

With negative images.

It's taboo for a black man

To give a smile

While trying not come off

Way too hostile

I realized my gift

Is writing words into actions

Always trying to please people

And give them satisfaction

I'm ready to live a life

With no pressure

I split myself into thirds

And ready to put them back together.

Maybe I should live in the moment

And being so sensitive

Taking action of my life

So I control the narrative.

Maybe my life is just a constant sideshow

For others' entertainment

Like a horror movie

In your family's basement.

Maybe I write poetry to connect

So my words won't be forgot

Trying to reach a higher power

Laying in a field of forget-me-nots.

Hanging up a tapestry

Of my family tree

Displaying it boldly

For everyone to see

With the strongest roots,

Branches out to be free

Together in love's hold

Our family's story, forever told

To my children and theirs

Our future is bright

Full of love and comfort

Surrounded by so much light.

When my hands get like my grandfather's

And not any sooner

My words will manifest

As I write my own future

ABOUT THE AUTHOR

VoShawn White is a poet, writer and author.

He enjoys traveling, gardening and music.

His fiction book, *Vivid Color* will be released later in life.

THANK YOU FOR THE SUPPORT

Mom

Jesse

Saniyah

Rebekah Bunting

Anne Elise Roop

Kellie Litvak

Quinton Thornton

Kaylee Jones

Alexis Ryder

Sebrena Williamson

Lindsay Dunn

Hannah Henderson

Courtney & Reggie Brown

Mariah, Kimberly & Iris

Sherwen White

Amiee Brydges

Elizabeth, Jon & Melanie

anyone whoever believed in me

You

Made in the USA
Columbia, SC
23 November 2024